LIVING UNAFRAID

BRAD ELMITT

WWW.LIVINGUNAFRAID.COM

Foreword

We are called to fear God but not man. And we are called to victory over the emotion of fear despite the obstacles that must be overcome. Brad Elmitt has captured not only the crippling emotion of fear but a biblical response that will engage you and equip you to take back the territory that the enemy has stolen. His passion to equip his generation and those of his legacy are a great encouragement to all who are teachable and willing to embrace the fear they encounter. Brad gives us the battle plan to walk through the eye of the storm with the power of the Holy Spirit reclaiming the territory that has been stolen. Read this book and pass it on to someone who needs courage spoken into their hearts and spirits. You will not be disappointed.

Dr. Gary Rosberg

Co-Founder, America's Family Coaches

Co-Author, 6 Secrets to a Lasting Love

TRIBUTE TO HANK

Life holds many mysteries. But few are more intriguing than the impact one person has on another – often without notice until some later time, some later place. Hank Evans is one of those people for me. Unfortunately, I'm unable to thank him in person as his life was cut short due to an untimely accident in 2014. It was the summer before Hank's junior year in high school when he died of a head injury at the age of 17.

Prior to that summer, my association with Hank was limited to exchanging "Hellos" in the hallways of the church we both attended. Oddly enough, I don't ever recall having a meaningful conversation with Hank, but I do have a vivid memory of him roaming the halls at church with a big smile on his face and one or more friends by his side. With the broad physical stature of the football lineman that he was, Hank was hard to miss. You may wonder how, with such limited interaction, could this young man impact my life? The answer is quite simple. Hank gave me the precious gift of encouragement and a vote of confidence to press on with a calling to share with others God's great command of "Do not be afraid." The best part is, Hank gave this gift by just being Hank, and living unafraid.

Six months before his death, Hank was among a large group of students attending an FCA (Fellowship of Christian Athletes) huddle at Johnston High School. I happened to be the speaker that night and my message included a challenge to the young listeners to ask themselves what their lives would be like if they were truly fearless and lived their lives unafraid. At the end of the talk, I offered everyone a black wristband with a white de-bossed message: THE GREAT COMMAND – DO NOT BE AFRAID. Along with most everyone else, Hank took one and immediately snapped it around his wrist. I'm sure many of those students removed their wristband within a few days, but Hank never did. In fact, he never took it off and was wearing it the day of his accident many months later.

But that's not all Hank did – he took to heart the challenge I presented that winter evening. According to his parents, Clint and Lori, Hank boldly shared his faith with friends and invited many to join him on Sunday nights at church for youth group. Wherever he went, he was connected with everyone and everything, exhibiting the zeal of a fearless spirit.

When learning this about Hank, his story was the nudge and encouragement I needed to follow through with my plans to write a short book, which to that point had stalled. Not only was Hank the inspiration I needed to finish my writing, but he also provided a valuable reminder and life lesson. Simply put, we don't always know what impact our words and actions will have on others, but we need to be mindful that God puts people in our lives intentionally, not by accident. For that reason, it's appropriate this book be dedicated to Hank Evans.

THIS PICTURE CAPTURES A MOMENT WHEN HANK'S FATHER CLINT WAS HOLDING ON TO HIS SON'S HAND IN THE HOSPITAL, JUST BEFORE RELEASING HIM INTO THE HANDS OF HANK'S HEAVENLY FATHER.

Contents

INTRODUCTION

It wasn't until I reached my mid-40s, in the midst of facing a period of unemployment, when I developed a keen awareness of how fear was such a dominant force in my life. Through this growing revelation, it became apparent just how frequently I second-guessed myself, doubted decisions and was simply afraid to act on opportunities as they arose.

The simple truth is, we're faced with opportunities every day. A few we encounter may indeed be critical, and on occasion, even life-changing. The truth is, many are simply common circumstances that pass through our lives almost without notice. While not seeming to be very significant at the time, collectively they shape who we are and who we will become. To provide a little more clarity, here are a few everyday tendencies many can relate to, which may help bring to light our human nature of living fearfully instead of fearlessly.

1. Difficulty in making simple decisions, such as which item to purchase or where to eat.

2. Not answering a question in a group setting when you know the correct response.

3. Regularly replaying in your mind conversations with people after they happen.

4. Not initiating a greeting or brief conversation with someone you know in a public place.

5. Disconnecting a phone call after you already dialed the number.

6. Not trying something you've never done before, even though there is no risk or danger.

7. Avoid sharing your faith because you worry about the reaction or the questions you may get.

8. Not sharing your idea or suggestion in a group setting because of what others may think.

9. Avoid confronting someone who needs to hear your loving concern or correction.

10. Not listening to the Holy Spirit's nudging to invite, serve or reach out to someone.

While I considered myself to be highly functional and a very capable individual, I was haunted by the question of what would my life be like if I was truly unafraid – to be fearless instead of fearful. If asked another way, how would my life be different today if I fully recognized every relationship and every opportunity God intentionally placed before me? Unfortunately, there are countless situations that, in the past, I wastefully discarded out of fear.

With the realization my life would have noticeably more meaning and alignment with God's will if I followed His command to not be afraid, I felt led to do two things. The first was to make this an area of personal growth and development. This would hopefully keep me from repeating the same mistakes of my past, while optimizing the future that God has planned for me. The other was to encourage others, from family and friends to those I've not yet met, to be more mindful of the choices they make that are driven by fear, instead of by their faith.

Both of these reasons prompted me to write this book that raises awareness on how crippling fear can be in our lives. From the smallest decisions to the largest, I felt the need to help equip people to live fearlessly instead of fearfully, so they can experience all the joys and blessings God has in store for them. However, there was a slight problem...the fear of writing a book! Actually, it's multiple fears – from the fear of investing countless hours on something that may never be published, to the fear of being woefully unqualified for such an endeavor due to lack of credentials, experience and skill. After all, I'm not even an avid reader, so what makes me think I could write a book that others will want to read?

All of these very valid considerations weighed heavily on my mind and served as effective barriers that kept me from taking the plunge. What made the difference now? It was a combination of experiences that ranged from tragedies to opportunities, but clearly the most influential was the continuous prompting of the Holy Spirit and a desire to "walk my talk" and be obedient to His calling. And besides, with God on my side, the same God who used a stuttering Moses to lead Israel out of Egypt, who could be against me? Bottom line, if God wants to bless the message within these pages, He will. Not even my own ineptitude can get in the way. Thank goodness!

This book is intended to be an easy read and one that resonates with readers of every age and stage of life. What it isn't, however, is a book to address the very real phobias that people unfortunately deal with in their everyday lives. While I wish I could help everyone deal with the many types of fears that impact so many lives today, I simply cannot. So if you fight a paralyzing fear over high places, small spaces or public speaking, my only hope is this material can serve as a reminder that everyone faces fear in varying degrees. Keep your eyes on the Lord because He is a powerful remedy.

I've written this book with three objectives in mind. The first is bringing awareness to how fear robs us from experiencing God's many blessings. The second is to challenge you to examine, with clear intention, how fear is impacting your life. And the third is to better equip you with the power to overcome fear.

To do this, I've provided a collection of biblical and personal applications of how fear can have significant consequences on both the seemingly small choices, as well as larger decisions we make throughout any given day. With each application, you will have the opportunity to reflect with greater awareness the role that fear played on your day and why. By the time you have read through this book, my hope is you will be more aware, ready and willing to live a fearless-driven life so you can experience all the joy that God desires for you.

1

THE LOVE LETTER

Genesis 15:1 (The Lord to Abram)

*After this, the word of the Lord came to Abram in a vision: "**Do not be afraid**, Abram. I am your shield, your very great reward."*

When I think of a love letter, an array of thoughts come to mind that go back to my days in junior high when we passed folded-up notebook paper in classrooms or hallways to the current crush-of-the-week. Then years later, during my first year in college, I remember sending love letters to my high school sweetheart who was attending school in another state. But the most memorable love letter that I received was from my father after I graduated from Iowa State University.

He wasn't what you'd consider an active communicator and, like many of his generation, dad was a man of few words. So when he did speak, of course I listened. And when he did write, which was only this one time that I remember, I read it with much curiosity and anticipation. His intent was not lost on me. He wrote this letter to formally communicate what was important to him – and what he wanted to impress upon me at that time in my life.

I still remember the first time I read this hand-written letter. Alone in my room, I was torn. Part of me wanted to slowly soak up each word, pondering every thought. Another side of me wanted to rush through it to find out what he wanted to say to me, to understand its purpose and release the wisdom therein. Of course, I read it several times and realized the one central theme that became so clear throughout this priceless love letter from father to son, was that he believed in me. Maybe you've had a similar experience when you received a valuable letter or note, and while you don't want to miss a word, you are incredibly anxious to uncover its meaning.

This love letter from my father was a gift in itself, which I still have and reference on occasion since his passing over 20 years ago. But this letter was actually written to inform me of a gift he wanted to give me for making it through college. Not only was it unexpected, but I also felt undeserved. Later, when expressing this feeling of undeserved appreciation, he simply smiled and said, "I know, but your mom and I love you and we want you to have this."

However, there was more to this letter than simply telling me about some unexpected spending money. This was my father's way of expressing his love and belief in me. I know this because these messages were repeated throughout the letter. Just like anything else that a parent wants to stress or emphasize with their children, deep and caring feelings are best reinforced through repetition.

I hope you have written and received a special love letter in your life because sharing thoughts and feelings with someone significant is priceless. However, there is one love letter that is the greatest of all. We know it as the Bible, and it has been changing lives for many centuries. Simply put, it's a very personal message from our heavenly father to all of us, His earthly children. And just like any parent who desperately wants to share with a child that which is vitally important and worthy, there are key messages that God reinforces through the Bible.

So what important thoughts does our heavenly father want to impress upon us as His children? Well, there is one command that is given more than any other in the Bible, and it doesn't contain the word "love." If you haven't guessed it yet, based on the title of this book, the command is "Do not be afraid." While it depends on which version of the Bible you are reading, these specific words have been identified nearly 100 times, which is why I refer to it as the great command. Please understand, I'm not referring to the great commission or the greatest commandment. Based simply on how many times it appears in scripture, the phrase, "Do not be afraid" is arguably the great command given by God, our heavenly father, through His love letter, the Bible.

So why would God do that? Why would God use a love letter to remind us more than any other message or command to "Do not be afraid?" I think it's important to always understand the "Why?" behind anything we are asked... or commanded to do. And, is this a command we should consider doing once in a while, or more broadly as a way to live? As for me and my house, I clearly view this command as a way to live. Let's go back to addressing the why. I believe, and respectfully submit to you for consideration, there are three key drivers behind God's intentional desire to express this command more than any other.

The first is He made us and He knows how we are wired. We are creatures filled with self-doubt and fear. We are obsessed with what others think of us, even more so than how we think of ourselves. We easily fall into the trap of thinking first of the worst-case scenario instead of the best-case outcome. We are all too familiar with our shortcomings and faults instead of recognizing our gifts and talents. We are easily reminded of our failures instead of our successes.

The second reason why God commands us to not be afraid is because He knows that we cannot come close to receiving all the blessings He has planned for us if we are held captive by our own fear and self-doubt. God tells us in Jeremiah 29:11 that He has a plan for us, plans to prosper, plans to give us hope and a future. Well, guess who's the only one who can get in the way of all that God has in store for us? You guessed it...us! And guess what emotion keeps us from being all that we can be, and blessing all those who God puts in our path? Right again...fear!

So what's the third piece to the "why" puzzle? I think it's as simple as God addressing the scary chapters of life. And of course, if not currently in the eye of a storm, we will be at some point. That's when we need to trust in Him, keeping our eyes solidly fixed on Him instead of the waves of life that buffer against us. The world we live in can be very hard and cruel, and at times circumstances can feel painfully unfair. God, of course, knows this and hopes we'll allow Him to love and prepare us.

Key Takeaways:

- God, our heavenly father, in His love letter, the Bible, clearly commands us, "Do not be afraid."
- He does this because He knows how we are wired and that we're filled with fear and self-doubt.
- And God knows we can't possibly be all that He has planned for us if we are afraid.

TIME OF REFLECTION:

When was the last time you were afraid to say or act on something?

What could have been the consequence if this didn't go well?

What could have potentially happened if this went really well?

How did you feel following this moment?

Heavenly Father, thank You for giving me another day to glorify You and to be a blessing to those You put in my path. Lord, may this day be more about You and less about me. I pray that Your Holy Spirit overflows within me and washes away my love for self and instead redirects my focus on You and the people You have specifically appointed to stand before me.

2

GLORIFYING GOD!

Genesis 46:3 (God to Jacob)

*"I am God, the God of your father," he said. "**Do not be afraid** to go down to Egypt, for I will make you into a great nation there."*

I believe that when we live a fearless life through our faith in Christ, we are glorifying God in a way that makes our heavenly father most pleased. In my mind, I can picture a brilliant smile that makes the angels shade their eyes. I'm a proud papa of my three children and I know when I see the face of another father beaming with glory over the triumph of his son or daughter. It is fair to say that any parent reading this would quickly agree some of their greatest moments or memories involve the achievements of their children. Which begs the question, would our heavenly father feel any differently about His children?

Let me share a setting that illustrates my point about bringing glory to God through our faith and trust in Him. Think back with me to either your own personal experience or a scene that you have observed at the local swimming pool. It's a hot summer day and over toward the deep end is a young boy standing at the side of the pool with his toes desperately gripping the concrete edge.

In the water, just a few feet away and facing the child paralyzed by fear, is dad with an affirming smile and outstretched arms. At stake is one of the more defining moments in the relationship between father and son. Dad is in the water encouraging his child to forget five-year-old logic and jump into water that is clearly over his head and deep enough to completely engulf him upon impact.

Here's what dad is saying as his son stands at the edge with quivering legs and arms crossed in a defying posture: "It's OK, go ahead and jump, I'll be right here for you if you need me. You know I wouldn't let anything happen to you." At this point the knobby knees slightly bend and the arms unlock to begin a hesitating swing as if to achieve maximum lift. However, the little boy's mind starts to wonder just how deep the water really is…what if dad doesn't get there in time…will he sink into the abyss never to be found? Besides the water is very cold and it feels good standing in the warm sun.

Dad can see the hesitation setting in and says, "Son, look at me, I want your attention!" Dad smiles. "You need to trust me! Jump and I'll be right here to lift you up." The father is insistent his son take this leap of faith because he knows how wonderful and extraordinary the experience will be, not to mention how critical this step is in learning to swim, which leads to the enjoyment of so many other water activities.

So what happens? The son finally musters up enough courage to jump, or actually step, into the deep water. Dad is right there with open arms ensuring it's a positive experience. And, oh what an experience it is! As the young child is lifted out of the water, their eyes lock with excitement and their faces greet one another with a wide-open smile. The boy shouts, "Wow, that was awesome dad…let's do it again!"

What follows is a series of leaps that move farther and farther from the edge and the father. And instead of dad lifting the son out of the water, the splurging confidence grows to the point where the young child floats to the top, thrashing his way toward the pool's edge. Off to the side is dad bursting with pride knowing his son is experiencing one of life's great pleasures and he is well on his way to enjoying the splendor that swimming has to offer. Best of all, it brings tremendous joy to the father knowing this accomplishment was possible only because his son was willing to fully trust him.

Maybe this pool scene brings back a personal memory for you as either the child or the parent. In either case, it is a clear illustration of our current relationship with our heavenly father and the ongoing battle between our fear and our faith. If this resonates with you, let me take it one step further with a daily application that's actually quite simple. It goes like this. Each morning as you start your day, picture your heavenly father greeting you with His outstretched arms, calling your name while smiling and saying, "Look at me and trust me. I will never leave you nor forsake you. Be strong and courageous. Do not be afraid or discouraged for I will be with you wherever you go." (Joshua 1:5, 1:9) "For I know the plans I have for you. Plans to prosper you and not to harm you, plans to give you hope and a future." (Jeremiah 29:11)

If you have ever wondered what God's plan is for you or where all the prosperity is that seems to allude you, ask yourself one revealing question: Do I live my life in a way that is obedient to His instruction and fearless in following His will? In other words, are you still standing on the edge of life's pool, weighing the risk and reward of jumping in? And, if you're not willing to take that step of faith, how can you experience the splash, the splendor and the all-encompassing joy our Lord has planned for you?

It's worth noting that each fearless act may not require the same level of bravery as jumping into the deep end of the pool for the first time. Keeping in mind God's plan, by taking a small step that is simply outside our comfort zone, we may be arranging the building blocks for bigger and better things to come. For the young child who just conquered the fear of jumping into water over his head, this may lead to swimming to the platform in the middle of the pool, going down the water slide, diving off the board, making the swimming team, or maybe even saving someone from drowning some day. While we may take this hypothetical progression for granted, it does illustrate the ripple affect our choices make in God's plan for our lives.

Another way to look at it is through a short series of questions and answers that begins with: Why did God create us? In it's simplest form, I believe the answer is to glorify Him. Well then, how do we glorify Him? How about by making a difference, doing what He created us to do. So, how do we make a difference by being Christ-like and a blessing to others? By living unafraid! And how do we live unafraid? Through our faith in God who created us!

One of my favorite life mottos is "Make a difference." The way I see it, if I'm not making a difference, in whatever endeavor I'm involved with, it forces me to wonder what I'm doing there? I certainly wasn't created for the purpose of just filling a space in my employer's office, a seat at a meeting or a spot on the team. No, I was created, just as we all were, to make a difference. As a father, when one of my kids began a new activity or started a game, I would encourage them to "make a difference." And, there is no doubt in my mind that our heavenly father is encouraging us to do the same.

When God witnesses his children seeking Him first and choosing faith over fear, He is glorified. If your heart desires to glorify God, and if you desire to live a life filled with all that God has planned for you, be fearless and your faith in Christ will lead you to incredible things.

KEY TAKEAWAYS:

- Our heavenly father has his arms stretched out toward us saying, "Trust me and jump!"
- Until we jump, we will never fully experience the joy of God's plan for our lives.
- When God sees his children seeking Him first and choosing faith over fear, He is glorified.

Time of Reflection:

Do you still find yourself standing on the pool's edge, paralyzed by fear?

When you are paralyzed by fear, are you lacking trust in God, yourself or someone else?

When was the last time you jumped into the deep end or took a risk?

How did you feel following this moment?

Heavenly Father, I'm reminded that You created me for Your glory and my heart desires to glorify You and please You in a way that brings a smile upon Your face of Holy grace. With Your strong and steady arms reaching out to catch me when I trust You enough to jump, what can I possibly fear, but fear itself?

3

FEAR VS. FAITH

Deuteronomy 1:21 (The Lord to Israel)

*See, the Lord your God has given you the land. Go up and take possession of it as the Lord, the God of your ancestors, told you. **Do not be afraid**; do not be discouraged.*

Think of it as good vs. evil, or day vs. night – every person's fear faces direct opposition from their faith. These two driving forces within us all are at constant odds against one another. Many times, they do battle at a subconscious level; other times, they are actively at war throughout the waking moments of our days.

As human beings we are made with a limited capacity. So when these opposing forces compete to occupy and control our thoughts, they in turn, direct our actions. It is important that we establish a baseline premise that if a person is controlled by their fear, they likely have very little faith. Conversely, if a person is guided by a very deep faith, that faith will ultimately suppress any fear or doubt that may exist. Simply put, when one increases and fills more of our being, the other decreases and becomes less of who we are.

Below is a simple visual to illustrate this relationship between our faith and fear. When our life is filled with faith, as represented by vertical lines on the left, our faith is a dominant influence, leaving little room for fear – allowing us to live fearlessly. On the contrary, when faith becomes a smaller part of our life, as represented by the vertical lines towards the right, we allow fear to take control – and we become more fearful.

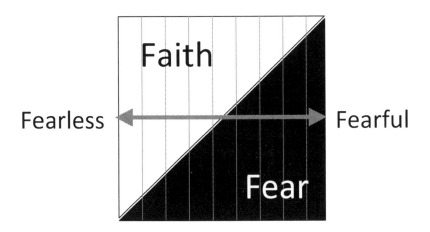

The Bible is filled with many stories intended to teach us through our mind's eye using visual depictions of key messages. In Matthew 14, there's a very powerful example that addresses the conflict between fear and faith. Jesus has finished feeding the 5,000 with just five loaves of bread and two fish. You may recall the setting as He instructs the disciples to get into a boat and go on ahead of Him to the other side of the lake to Capernaum, while He dismisses the crowd.

Once alone, Jesus spent time praying on the mountainside until nightfall, then He set out to meet his disciples – by walking on the water! When the disciples saw Him approach their boat, they were terrified because they thought Jesus was a ghost. Seeing they were afraid, Jesus said, "Take courage! It is I. Don't be afraid."

Arguably the most fearless and spontaneous of the disciples, Peter shouts, "Lord, if it's you, tell me to come to you on the water." Which makes me wonder who was more shocked by this response, Peter or the other 11 in the boat? I can't help but wonder if Peter may have asked himself, "What did I just say? Did that really come out of my mouth? What was I thinking?" If so, I could certainly relate to such a predicament. Regardless, Peter showed unimaginable courage, crawled over the edge of the boat, and fearlessly walked on the water toward Jesus. While it doesn't really matter, we don't know how many steps he actually took, but it was enough for him to make his way toward Jesus.

Here's what does matter – Peter took his eyes off Jesus. When he did, imagine the sense of panic! The wind. The waves. The sinking feeling…literally! Peter began to go down not because the waves were overtaking his balance, but because the weight of doubt and fear gripped him like an anchor tied to his feet. I believe the wind that Peter encountered represents the same type of winds that confront us today in the form of past failures, time demands, selfishness, critical spirits and, of course, self-doubt, to name a few.

So what does Peter do next? He cries out to Jesus, "Lord, save me!" Not only is it difficult to be critical of Peter because he so courageously got out of a boat and walked on water, but he also deserves credit for quickly recognizing his one and only savior. What a great lesson and example this provides as Peter didn't try to fix it on his own or make an attempt to get back to the boat. He turned his eyes back on Jesus who reached out his hand and caught him.

If we were keeping score with a play-by-play recap of what just transpired over the course of just a few moments, the highlights would look something like this:

FEAR WINS WHEN...	**FAITH WINS WHEN...**
The disciples were terrified thinking Jesus was a ghost	
	Peter offers to meet Jesus on the water
	Jesus calls Peter to do the unthinkable, and Peter does it
Peter sees the wind, becomes afraid and begins to sink	
	Peter cries out to Jesus to save him, and he is saved

Final score: Peter's faith triumphs over fear, but only after turning his attention back to Jesus.

But this story isn't over as Jesus says something to Peter that seems a little harsh by most human standards – "You of little faith, why did you doubt?" Frankly, if I were Peter at that point, I would have been looking for a high-five or a "that-a-boy" pat on the back from Jesus for doing something I thought was rather courageous and extraordinary. Instead of giving Peter some nurturing words of encouragement, Jesus chose to impress upon Peter that with much faith, anything is possible.

What if you really believed this? It's time to be honest. It's time to ask yourself, "What would my life be like if my faith in Christ, and my trust in His plan and His promise of eternal life rang so loud and true in me, that fear of failure, fear of opinion, or fear of embarrassment become a hollow and distant echo? If you are wanting more out of your life, if you are tired of facing the "what ifs?" or missed opportunities, stop worrying about the wind and start looking at your Lord who not only wants you to walk on water , but to go the distance in reaching your full potential!

Matthew 14:30-31

30 But when Peter saw the wind, he was afraid and, beginning to sink, cried out, "Lord, save me!" 31 Immediately Jesus reached out his hand and caught him. "You of little faith," he said, "why did you doubt?"

KEY TAKEAWAYS:

- Fear and faith are two driving forces within each person that are constantly at odds fighting for control. When we feed one, the other starves.
- Peter was fearless as he got down from the boat to walk on water, but when he took his eyes off Jesus and saw the wind, he became afraid.
- Jesus tells Peter and each of us that a little faith gets us just so far and His desire and plans for us are greater than we can imagine, if we have much faith in Him.

Time of Reflection:

Have you ever recognized the relationship between your level of fear and faith? If so, when?

What distracts you most from your relationship with God?

What's the best way for you to feed your relationship with God?

How would you describe what you think is God's will for your life?

Heavenly Father, I am weak when the winds are blowing and the waves are crashing. Fortify my heart and fix my eyes on You. Only You are my true shield to fend off all fear and feed my fragile faith. Fill me so full of Your love that fear has no place in my mind, heart or soul.

4

FEARING GOD

Exodus 20:20

*Moses said to the people, "**Do not be afraid**. God has come to test you, so that the fear of God will be with you to keep you from sinning."*

The Bible makes multiple references about fearing God. What? After all this talk about being fearless and not being afraid, it's important to clarify what it means to fear God or to be a "God-fearing" person. If God truly loves us, if He is our heavenly father who forgives our sins, why should we fear Him?

When fear is a governing influence in a person's life, I believe it can be grouped into three broad categories: The fear of things (often called phobias), the fear of man and the fear of God. Because we live in a society that loves lists, especially top 10 lists, it's easy to find a listing of the things people fear most. Here are two short lists of common fears that fall under the first two categories:

Fear of Things or Phobias	**Fear of Man or People**
Public Speaking	Intimacy and Commitment
Heights or Flying	Failure and Rejection
Enclosed Spaces	Embarrassment/Humiliation
Snakes and Spiders	Judgment
Needles and Germs	Loneliness

Chances are, you can identify to some degree with many of these examples, as they can be very powerful influences in a person's life. But where does the third type of fear, the fear of God, fit into all this and what does it mean? Simply put, I believe it speaks to who God is and who we can become!

Let's take a look into the scriptures for some insight. To fear the Lord is to be humble with a reverent heart, kneeling before God who is holy, almighty, righteous, all-knowing and all-powerful. And when we regard our God in this way, we gain a clearer picture of ourselves. It's only when we recognize who God is, will we be able to see His way and His plan for us, with the wisdom to follow His lead. Psalm 25:12 reads, "Who then is the man that fears the Lord? He will instruct him in the way chosen for him." And Job 28:28 says, "The fear of the Lord – that is wisdom, and to shun evil is understanding." In other words, the starting point to finding real wisdom is to fear the Lord.

From a parental perspective, Moses reminds the Israelites in Exodus 20:20 that the fear of God will help keep them from sinning. Just like a child fears the punishment of their father when they have misbehaved, so Christians must be mindful of their sinful behavior and their heavenly father's judgment. Without a healthy respect for the Lord, founded in both fear and love, we know we're not likely to turn from our sinful ways. It reminds me of when I was a child. Whenever I misbehaved for my mother, I dreaded my father's arrival home from work or the dinner conversation that followed. My anxiety was not only driven by my fear of punishment, (which was never physical), but also my fear of disappointing a man I dearly loved.

Psalm 112 begins with "Blessed is the man who fears the Lord, who finds great delight in his commands." Then this passage continues to identify all the blessings awarded to those who fear the Lord, which includes upright children, wealth and riches, and a righteous reputation lasting forever. Then in verses 7-8 it reads, "He will have no fear of bad news; his heart is steadfast, trusting in the Lord. His heart is secure, he will have no fear; in the end he will look in triumph on his foes." To me, that sounds like some pretty good benefits for fearing the Lord and following His commands.

In Isaiah 8:11-13, the Lord spoke to Isaiah and said "Do not fear what they fear, and do not dread it. The Lord Almighty is the one you are to regard as holy, He is the one you are to fear."

Here is the bottom line, in Isaiah 57:11, which gets back to the point that our God is a jealous God when he says, "Whom have you so dreaded and feared that you have been false to me and have neither remembered me nor pondered this in your hearts?" Ouch! This particular passage is a reminder that if there is one thing to fear, it's the mistake of fearing man over fearing God. If we are true to God (not false), and if we remember Him (not ignore), we can be all that God has planned for us and all our unwarranted fears can rest in the palm of our all-knowing and all-powerful heavenly father.

1 Samuel chapter 15 captures a life-change decision by Saul when

he chooses to fear his men over obeying his God – the same one who anointed him king. In particular, rather than follow God's instructions to totally destroy all living creatures of an enemy he just conquered, Saul gave in to his men who wanted to keep some of the best livestock. While this may seem a mild offense, Samuel informs Saul in verse 15:26, that because he rejected the word of the Lord, the Lord has rejected him as king over Israel.

While Saul explains to Samuel that he was "afraid" of his men, it makes me wonder if Saul truly feared for his wellbeing or if he was more fearful about his popularity? When I think of the choices I make for the sake of "popularity" the lesson here really hits home. Simply put, it doesn't matter what a person's stature is, even that of a king, God's judgment matters more than man's.

Who is someone in your life that you fear more than God? Is this person a classmate, coach or teacher? Maybe this person is an acquaintance, work associate or neighbor? Does your fear stem from what this person might say or do? Could they possibly inflict physical, emotional, or financial harm? Frankly speaking, these are all very real fears that are difficult to ignore and weigh heavily on the choices we make in relation to the potential threat. When we do respond to these fears and choose a path of least resistance or reluctant compliance, it can easily be justified as a simple matter of common sense.

If you are familiar with the Bible story of Joshua who led the Israel army in the fall of Jericho, you may recall the role of Rehab, a lowly prostitute and citizen of this fortified city. In short, what we learn about Rehab is she feared God more than the king of Jericho. By hiding and protecting the two spies Joshua sent to scout out the city, and misleading the king of their whereabouts, she risked everything out of her reverent fear of God. I have to believe Rehab fully considered what the king of Jericho might have done to her and her family if he had learned the truth.

Just think how easy it would have been for Rehab to expose the two spies from Israel and become a hero among her community and king. Instead, her fear of God not only put her life at risk, but also the lives of her entire family. Instead of choosing comfort, improved stature and possibly fame, Rehab chose to fear God over the fear of man.

KEY TAKEAWAYS:

* Fearing God is about recognizing who God is and who we can become.
* Wisdom and understanding begins with fearing the Lord.
* Many blessings are available to those who fear the Lord and delight in His commands.
* The one mistake we must avoid is fearing the judgment of man more than the judgment of God.

TIME OF REFLECTION:

When was the last time you feared man's judgment more than you feared God's judgment and what was the outcome?

What things do you fear most and how could they limit God's plan for you?

Heavenly Father, forgive me when I fear the judgment of family, friends and even acquaintances over my respectful fear of Your righteous and almighty power. My desire is to know You more and to see the path You have laid before me as I delight in obediently following Your commands.

5

FEARLESS VS. FEARFUL

Daniel 10:12 (The Lord to Daniel)

*He said to me, "**Do not be afraid**, Daniel. Since the first day that you set your mind to gain understanding and to humble yourself before your God, your words were heard, and I have come in response to them."*

One of my all-time favorite passages comes from John 9 in which Jesus heals a man who was born blind. While there are many valuable lessons embedded in this story, at its core, a man who was discarded by his parents years before, puts the Pharisees to shame with a simple but fearless testimony. It goes like this...

Outside the temple grounds, Jesus sees a man, blind from birth. Due to his defect, it is likely this man was discarded by his family, having to fend for himself on the streets by begging for food and spare change. He was so pathetic the disciples questioned Jesus about the cause of such hardship asking, "Rabbi, who sinned, this man or his parents, that he was born blind?"

Jesus answered by saying neither, explaining he was born blind so God may be glorified. He then proceeded to heal the man, using him as a human instrument of God. Making mud with his saliva and dirt, Jesus placed it on the man's eyes and instructed him to go to the Pool of Siloam to wash. Consider this – based on the scriptures, the man obeyed without question, gained his sight, then went home without further contact with Jesus.

After hearing this amazing story, and knowing this miracle took place on the Sabbath, the people rushed the man to the Pharisees, the religious leaders who served as the governing body. The man was interrogated. Who? What? Why? And when the man gave his answers, the Pharisees were confused and divided. To get to the bottom of what happened, they sent for the man's parents to testify on his behalf.

It shouldn't come as a surprise, since his parents had already abandoned their son long ago, they opted to "plead the 5th" and would only confirm he was their son. Instead of rejoicing over the gift of sight given to their son, the fearful parents answered the Pharisees by stating their son "is of age and can speak for himself." Only concerned about themselves, they were afraid that saying anything more would be held against them and would result in expulsion from the synagogue.

Unlike his parents, the lowly man who was just given his sight was unafraid. The Pharisees asked him a second time to testify against Jesus, saying, "Give glory to God, we know this Jesus is a sinner." He replied, "I don't know. One thing I do know, I was blind but now I see!" Then he proceeded to say, "I have told you already and you did not listen. Why do you want to hear it again? Do you want to become His disciples, too?" Well, you can imagine how the boldness of that question stung the Pharisees!

The man goes on to say, "We know that God does not listen to sinners. He listens to the godly man who does his will. Nobody has ever heard of opening the eyes of a man born blind. If this man were not from God, he could do nothing." The truth of this statement cut to the core of the hypocrisy displayed by the religious leaders, and they threw him out.

I think what is so amazing about this exchange is – a man who had never seen Jesus with his eyes, a man who had never rehearsed sharing his testimony, a man who had never previously spoken to the religious leaders, and a man who never received loving support from his parents – simply cuts the Pharisees off at the knees. And everybody knew it! He was totally out of his league facing off against the most well-spoken and educated men of Israel, yet his amazing faith in Jesus prevailed.

For me, what strikes at the core of my Christian walk is how many times over the years I was too afraid to share my faith in Christ, worried I may not have all the answers, or the words to eloquently support my beliefs. How many people has God put in my path expecting me to testify on His behalf? Instead, I bailed out because of my own petty insecurity. How many souls have I encountered who simply needed a few words of reassurance or to hear about God's glory? How rejected God must have felt each time I let my self-centered fear override my little faith.

But the story doesn't end with the beggar slaying a host of religious giants – it ends with the greatest honor given to only a handful of people in the history of mankind. When Jesus heard what happened, he looked for and found the lowly beggar, who testified on His behalf. I can only imagine the exchange as the Lord's eyes met the eyes that could now see, and how everything else around them fell silent as time stood still.

Have you ever wondered where God is? Why He's ignoring you? Why you feel so distant? Maybe He is also wondering why your faith is overwhelmed and suffocated by your fear about trivial things that don't really matter. What would happen if you lived a day where you were absolutely fearless through your faith in Christ? What would happen if every opportunity God put before you, the big and the small, was eagerly met with a fearless mindset?

Give it a try and start right now. He is waiting!

Key Takeaways:

- You don't need to have a polished testimony to be a witness for Jesus – just a fearless heart.
- When people (even your parents) are more worried about their stature and reputation than doing what is right, they are likely to act fearfully instead of fearlessly.
- If you are currently in a dark place and seeking the face of Jesus, be encouraged by the blind man's fearless witness – one so powerful that it moved Jesus to go find him.

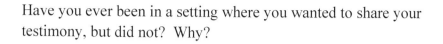

TIME OF REFLECTION:

Have you ever been in a setting where you wanted to share your testimony, but did not? Why?

When was the last time you chose not to act or speak, out of fear for your reputation, and why?

If someone asked you today how God has impacted your life, what would you say?

Heavenly Father, grant me a fearless heart over having a flawless testimony. Open my eyes to see opportunities to be a witness for You and to be a blessing to others. Allow only truth to be spoken from my limits with disregard to reputation, personal gain or social status.

6

POWER OF THE HOLY SPIRIT

John 14:26 (Jesus to the Disciples)

But the Advocate, the Holy Spirit, whom the Father will send in my name, will teach you all things and will remind you of everything I have said to you.

While on a walk with my wife and best friend of over 30 years, Lori and I were talking about how much has changed in the world over a relatively brief period of time. The conversation eventually shifted to the impact of technology and, between the two of us, we quickly agreed she tends to embrace change and innovation much more than I do. As we talked further, Lori encouraged me to be more progressive and let go of some of my traditional ways and thinking.

One such example, she reminded me, was my reluctance to convert from a traditional cell phone to the widely used "smart" phones that bring fingertip access to unlimited information. For a variety of reasons, I was very content using a phone that allowed me to simply talk and text. In addition to meeting my limited needs, it was small and fit comfortably in any pocket. While she won't admit it, I'm still convinced that Lori, who always checks the pockets before doing laundry, purposely washed my four-year-old flip phone! Accident or not, because of my stubborn nature and resistance to change, my loving wife intervened in order to help me experience the new world of smart phones.

I believe people are reluctant to change and many are truly afraid of it. Maybe you can identify with one or the other, and as a result, have a very keen awareness of the uncertainty that comes with change. Regardless of how difficult change may be, it's generally accepted that people can and do change. For some, it may be the type of change that happens over long periods of time. Others may experience a life-changing moment that drastically alters their outlook immediately.

Think about this – over the course of history, has there ever been a more significant change recorded among men than when the disciples received the Holy Spirit? As a group, they were arguably a collection of bumbling misfits, a self-centered collection of shallow thinkers and fearful souls. In Mark 14:50, it clearly states that every one of Jesus' disciples deserted him and fled the garden of Gethsemane after Judas identified Jesus with a kiss and Peter drew his sword in a panic. There are plenty of examples throughout the gospels of the disciples just not "getting it," even while living in the daily presence of Jesus Christ. The power of the Holy Spirit is a topic that can fill the pages of a book all by itself, but I would like to narrow the focus on Peter, the recognized leader among Jesus' followers.

Please understand, I'm certainly not suggesting Peter was a wimp as he was far more fearless than I will ever be. However, he was truly a different man after receiving the Holy Spirit. In Matthew 26 we read about Peter denying he even knows Jesus three different times while his Lord is being spit upon and struck in the face during questioning from the high priest. For review, the first time was in response to a servant girl, while sitting in the courtyard. The second time was near the gateway of the courtyard, and in response to another girl's question. Shortly there after, some people who were standing by Peter challenged him again, thinking his accent was a sure give away. Of course, it was at that moment the rooster crowed and Peter was reminded of Jesus telling him he would disown Him three times.

I find it interesting that in two of the three occasions when Peter quickly denied Jesus, it was in response to a girl, who certainly shouldn't have posed a threat to him. (This would make for a good trivia question that I believe few would answer correctly.) This speaks to how a lack of faith, even momentarily, feeds a person's fear as Peter's understanding and faith were clearly shaken at this point. When was the last time you heard the rooster crow? For example, while in a social setting or talking with another person, you reluctantly join in on a dishonoring discussion or you pass on an opportunity to show your faith or share your testimony. We all have experienced moments like this when we wish we had done things differently. But after receiving the Holy Spirit, Peter never denied Jesus the rest of his life…what a tremendous way to honor your Lord and Savior.

The opportunity for Peter's redemption came quickly after the Holy Spirit came upon the disciples on the day of Pentecost. In Acts 4, after Peter heals a crippled beggar, he and John were brought before the Sanhedrin for questioning. It reads in verses 8-10: "Then Peter, filled with the Holy Spirit, said to them: 'Rulers and elders of the people! If we are being called to account today for an act of kindness shown to a cripple and are asked how he was healed, then know this, you and all the people of Israel: It is by the name of Jesus Christ of Nazareth, whom you crucified but whom God raised from the dead, that this man stands before you healed.'" When the Sanhedrin saw Peter's boldness and lack of fear, they were astonished and released him.

The apostle Paul is rightfully credited for bringing the gospel to non-Jews. However, it's easy to overlook that Peter was the first who reached out to Gentiles. While today this may not seem like such a big deal and the natural thing to do, in Peter's time it defied the very core of Jewish law. It was a form of treason, surely to be judged harshly by his peers and everyone who mattered to him. Yet, with the conviction of the Holy Spirit and a fearless heart to do the Lord's work, Peter accepted the invitation to meet with the family and friends of Cornelius, a Roman army officer.

In Acts 10, we learn how Peter boldly shared the gospel in the home of Cornelius and upon hearing his words, the Holy Spirit came upon everyone who heard his message. Peter didn't stop here as a moral victory. In Acts 10:47 Peter said, "Can anyone keep these people from being baptized with water? They have received the Holy Spirit just as we have." Peter wanted to seal the deal by using this public act of faith to demonstrate equality among both Jews and Gentiles. Peter was so driven by the power of the Holy Spirit, he didn't worry about the harsh criticism he was sure to receive.

Upon his return to Judea, Peter was able to convince his critics (primarily the other apostles and fellow believers), telling them all what had happened and how the power of the Holy Spirit directed him in his understanding and actions. Hearing Peter's testimony, they had no further objections and praised God with new insight that even Gentiles can be chosen by God and receive the Holy Spirit. This realization, as an outcome of Peter going against traditional law as directed by the power of the Holy Spirit, became a significant turning point for the early church.

These are great reminders of the Holy Spirit's power, the same Holy Spirit that dwells within all believers. But wait a minute, if this is true, why don't we see more fruits of the Spirit in us? We will explore this further in the next chapter.

KEY TAKEAWAYS:

- People are naturally resistant to change, but the power of the Holy Spirit can change anyone.
- There was one defining moment that turned the fearful disciples into fearless apostles and that was the receiving of the Holy Spirit.
- When Peter denied Jesus three times, his fear level was at an all-time high because his faith and understanding of what was happening was at an all-time low.
- If the power of the Holy Spirit allowed Peter to change the coarse of the early Christian church, the Holy Spirit is more than capable of using you to impact the lives of others.

Time of Reflection:

What is something in your life that needs changing, but you've been unable to make this change on your own?

If you don't feel the power of the Holy Spirit working in your life, what barriers are keeping you from hearing and feeling His influence? Could it be sin, other idols, busyness...be honest!

Is there something the Holy Spirit is prompting you to do that could change lives forever?

Heavenly Father, may Your spirit fall fresh on me. Lord, fill me with courage and empower me to be all that You intended. May the power of Your Spirit be boldly evident in my life, leaving no doubt that I am Yours and You are my source of protection, my source of power and my savior.

7

BEING OBEDIENT

Genesis 26:24 (The Lord to Isaac)

*That night the Lord appeared to him and said, "I am the God of your father Abraham. **Do not be afraid**, for I am with you; I will bless you and will increase the number of your descendants for the sake of my servant Abraham."*

For much of my life, I've been driven by a desire to please my parents. And except for a few hiccups during my youth, when incredibly stupid ideas entered my under-developed brain, I was a pleaser who did all I could to be obedient to them. While spiritual faith was not a driving force in the make-up of our family, my sister and I were recipients of intentional teaching and modeling of good moral behavior. We were taught to understand the difference between right and wrong. So we both worked hard to give our parents plenty of reasons to be proud of us.

I'm sure many of you can relate to having a desire to be obedient to your parents, to your work supervisor or simply to the common laws that govern our society. When growing up, if my father asked me to do something around the house for him or for my mother, I was typically responsive to honor his request as an act of obedience and love for him. I even believed the quicker I was to follow through with the task, as close to perfection as possible, the greater my display of obedience and love. When my father spoke, I listened and obeyed.

What about in the workplace? When our boss or manager speaks to us with instructions, requests or suggestions, it would clearly seem in our best interest to follow through. Just like a child being obedient to a parent, a conscientious employee hopes to make a favorable impression with an employer or manager by responding promptly and precisely. By doing so, a hardworking and diligent employee over time earns credibility to receive more responsibility and, hopefully, an increase in salary.

This all seems very evident and straightforward, but it also begs the question: If God is the king of kings and reigns over our lives, and we've invited Him into our hearts to dwell within us, why do we ignore or override the voice of the Holy Spirit, our heavenly counselor? If I'm not mistaken, God didn't send the Holy Spirit to dwell within us because there wasn't any room in Heaven's Inn. Christ says specifically in John 14:26, "But the Counselor, the Holy Spirit, whom the Father will send in my name, will teach you all things and will remind you of everything I have said to you." Romans 8:26-27 goes on to say, "In the same way, the Spirit helps us in our weakness. We do not know what we ought to pray for, but the Spirit himself intercedes for us with groaning too deep for words. And he who searches our hearts knows the mind of the Spirit, because the Spirit intercedes for the saints in accordance with God's will." In other words, God speaks His wisdom and will for us through the Holy Spirit.

If the nudge that our heart feels or the voice our mind hears is that of the Holy Spirit, why do we ignore it so often? How many times have you felt an urge to reach out to someone, to provide an act of kindness, to share a new idea or to try something new, only to be afraid to act on it? I feel that such an occurrence is clear disobedience to the Lord who is guiding us to follow His will and plan for our prosperous and abundant lives.

I'm convinced that one of the areas the Holy Spirit stretches us most is in the area of sacrificial love, or unselfish acts of kindness. John reminds us in 1 John 3:23-24, "And this is his command: to believe in the name of his Son, Jesus Christ, and to love one another as he commanded us. Those who obey his commands live in him and he in them. And this is how we know that he lives in us: We know it by the Spirit he gave us." Unfortunately, I believe we all too often tune out the Spirit's voice of sacrificial love and kindness to listen to the self-centered sound of "what's in it for me." Sadly, the muzzle we frequently strap around the voice of the Holy Spirit is really an act of disobedience, driven by self-indulgence and an obsession for protecting one's self-interest.

So, how much more meaning and impact would our lives have, if we were not afraid to obey the guidance of the Holy Spirit? In Acts 2 we read about the day of Pentecost when the disciples received the Holy Spirit. From that day on, the cowardly band of followers became the most fearless men on earth, guided by the Holy Spirit, destined to change the history of mankind. I can't promise any of us are destined to change history. But, I will say with confidence, if you are unafraid and respond to the guidance of the Holy Spirit, you are destined to live a more fulfilled life that is aligned with God's glorious plan for you.

Key Takeaways:

- If we desire to be obedient, we need to be obedient to the Holy Spirit.
- The Holy Spirit calls us to be a blessing to others through sacrificial love.
- Consider the life-changing power of the Holy Spirit in the lives of the disciples and what is possible when we are obedient to its leading.

Time of Reflection:

Have you ever considered the ideas that come to your mind as the voice of the Holy Spirit?

Describe the last time you sensed the Holy Spirit leading you?

When you acted on the leading of the Holy Spirit, what was the outcome?

How would your life be different if you were obedient to God's leading?

Lord, I desire an obedient heart that is eager to hear Your voice. Call to me throughout this day and guide me as a lamp unto my feet with each step I take and every word I speak. Speak to me throughout this day so I may learn Your will and glorify Your name.

8

SHARING YOUR HEART

John 14:27 (Jesus to the Disciples)

*"Peace I leave with you; my peace I give you. I do not give to you as the world gives. Do not let your hearts be troubled and **do not be afraid**."*

When it comes to avoiding hard feelings or conflict, there's a longstanding nugget of advice that you may have heard at some point in your life. It goes something like this, in one form or another: "Some things are better off thought, but not said." While there is certainly some solid wisdom in these words, a strong case can also be made for saying things with love and speaking your heart. The sharing of one's heart can come in multiple forms, but I would like to focus on two that are oftentimes suppressed by fear. The first is to be transparent in key relationships and the other is to provide counsel to loved ones when they need to hear your insight.

A great place to start on transparency is acknowledging the need for a transparent heart with God. This statement may be a bit puzzling when you consider He knows our heart and He knows what we are thinking and feeling. However, this need for a transparent heart with God is an act on our part to intentionally surrender our fears and worries to the Lord. Until we continually submit our concerns, insecurities and fears through prayer, I truly believe it will be difficult, if not impossible, for us to feel released by the things of which we are most afraid.

In varying degrees, especially between men and women, God made us to be relational creatures. As we all know, some of us are just better equipped than others in making and nurturing sustainable relationships. A common trait for those who do excel in building meaningful, long-term relationships is a willingness to be transparent, without fear of sharing their heart. This is especially true for those important, intimate relationships in our lives, particularly between spouses, or with parents and children.

If you're a parent, when was the last time you wished that your son or daughter better understood how you felt about something or knew why you reacted the way you did to a specific situation? Maybe you were afraid to share your heart, worried about what they may think, or afraid they wouldn't understand, and think less of you. Isn't this relationship worth the risk?

Let's turn things around – when a child desires a more intimate relationship with a parent but struggles to get past the shallow exchanges. I would encourage you to not be afraid and share this desire with your parent, exhibiting your own transparency. When appropriate, ask loving questions about how they feel about topics or issues. Regardless of which side of the coin you are on, do not be afraid to share your heart or search the heart of loved ones.

What about you silent romantics out there, who currently have strong feelings for someone, but choose to keep things under "lock-and-key," submitting to fear instead of expressing your love? I truly believe this is something that becomes easier as one ages. But unfortunately for some, it's one of life's most heartbreaking moments when love passes by without a spoken word. Sharing with someone your feelings for them can be awkward for a moment – or two, but what a small price to pay in exchange for what may be a lifelong relationship. Besides, whether the feeling is mutual or not, at a bare minimum, you will have blessed someone with the knowledge they are admired or loved. Frankly, such a gift couldn't be more Christ-like. So "just do it" for love's sake!

I think one of the first signs of a struggling marriage is when a couple stops sharing what's on their hearts – their fears, pains and even joys. Unfortunately, the resulting alternative is when one of the spouses finds someone outside of the marriage who is open to hearing or sharing their feelings. Disaster isn't far away by this point. So it's a wonderful, healthy practice for couples to regularly carve out time to talk each day, but also to connect their souls by sharing their hearts. I've even heard of couples who make it a point to have undivided "talk time" at a specific time and place (as soon as they each get home each day, for example). By the way, did I mention these are happily married couples?

Men, because this is not in our DNA, it may be tempting just to wave the white flag and say, "Sorry, honey, that's just not me." If that's the case and you choose not to make the effort, is it because your wife and family aren't worth it, or are you just afraid she won't love the "real" you? Based on personal experience, I want to encourage you to not be afraid, because the act of sharing your heart will automatically lead to a connection with your wife that far exceeds the misguided fear of her "unfair" judgment.

Many of us live a life filled with regrets – some big, some small. But, one of the most haunting regrets I've heard about has to do with a person knowing they could have changed an unfortunate or even tragic outcome, but didn't intercede. It's painful knowing things may have turned out differently had fear or self-doubt not blocked someone from sharing their heart. After the fact, all the "what-ifs" seem embarrassingly silly and insignificant compared to the pain or loss resulting from a lack of action.

There are countless examples that come to mind and worth illustrating. For starters, what about all the adult and mature Christians who have a parent or loved one that doesn't know Jesus Christ as their Lord and Savior? Is it because the timing or setting never seemed right to share one's faith, to ask them where they stand, and if need be, to pray with them to ask Jesus into their life? Heartache will strike twice. The first time is when a loved one passes away leaving a tremendous void within the family; the second time occurs shortly thereafter when the uncertainty of a reunion in Heaven is questioned. One fearless discussion can change this situation. But it means dealing with the fear of rejection, the fear of not having all the answers and the fear of an awkward moment. If, and when, you find this situation at your footstep, share your heart with your loved one sooner than later because the eternal reward far exceeds the potential risk of a bruised ego.

For those of us who have children, we know parenting is the hardest endeavor we will ever undertake. This may be even more difficult for parents who struggle with being their child's friend versus being their parent. This seems to be particularly difficult for today's parents, especially those who may feel the guilt of not being around due to their career demands. As a result, rather than share concerns about who their kids are hanging out with, how they are spending their time, and the social choices they are making with drinking or dating, some parents are simply afraid of being rejected and not liked by their children. Unfortunately in these circumstances, the children are most likely acting out to get attention, hoping to hear their parent's heart, to know they are worth the difficult conversations. So if you suspect your kids are going down the wrong path, you are most likely right and you can't be afraid to share your heart by having the hard, but loving talks…even more than once!

While the act of sharing one's heart is not limited to adult conversations, it's certainly a skill that develops over time, and only improves with frequency. Regardless of your age, I believe we are all called to lovingly share what God has placed on our hearts when someone is in need – God is using us as a messenger to impact another life. When you have a child, parent, sibling or friend who is making poor choices and endangering themselves or someone else, why would you think God is calling someone other than you to intervene? It's really very simple. Avoid a life filled with regret, and follow God's nudging when he has placed something on your heart to lovingly share with another person, and do not be afraid!

Key Takeaways:

- If God has placed something on your heart to share with another person, He did it for a reason, so do not be afraid.
- A key to building meaningful relationships is a willingness to be transparent, to let people share the beauty of your heart.
- If you are in fellowship with the Lord, He will be using you to impact the lives of others.
- Avoid living with regrets over not sharing what's on your heart with people you care about.

TIME OF REFLECTION:

When were you afraid to share something that was on your heart, but you did it anyway?

How was the message you shared, received by the other person?

What could potentially be the outcome of you sharing your heart in this situation?

How did you feel following this exchange and was it worth taking the risk?

Heavenly Father, there is so much that goes unsaid that You have placed on my heart. Speak through me, Lord, when there are critical things I need to share with those I care deeply about. Give me the courage to speak truth, the wisdom to speak carefully and empathy to speak kindly and feel how my words are being received.

FACING YOUR GOLIATH

1 Samuel 12:20 (Samuel to Israel)

*"**Do not be afraid**," Samuel replied. "You have done all this evil; yet you do not turn away from the Lord, but serve the Lord with all your heart."*

I firmly believe that one of the main reasons the story of David and Goliath is so popular among Christians of all ages is not just because the underdog reins victorious, but because so many people find themselves facing a Goliath in their own lives. Today's Goliaths can take many forms, and while none of them are nine feet tall, they certainly seem just as formidable.

Your Goliath could be a bully at school or a manipulative associate in the workplace. Or maybe it's not a person at all, but takes the form of a relentless addiction that enslaves your soul and self worth. Then of course, there are some who are literally in a fight for their lives facing a serious disease or health concern. Regardless of what or who your Goliath is, there are lessons to be learned from David and his encounter with the giant Philistine.

Let's examine the scene when David arrives at the standoff between the Israelite and Philistine armies. Keep in mind he was there simply to deliver loaves of bread to his brothers, not to pick a fight or get revenge. (I can only wonder what David's father was thinking by sending his teenage son into a war zone?) But the situation quickly changed when David heard Goliath shouting insults against Israel, defying the armies of the living God.

I think it's interesting to note that when David started showing an interest in joining the battle, his first detractor was someone very close to him, David's older brother, Eliab. Do you have doubters or naysayers in your life who tend to discourage you in your efforts? If so, and their spirit is critical and jealous like that of David's brother, it may be better for you to turn your back on them, just as David did to Eliab.

As desperate as Saul was for a solution to take out Goliath, he too, was a doubter of David's ability and unbridled enthusiasm. Saul's response to David's offer to fight the giant was one of rejection, reminding him he was only a boy. David doesn't take "no" for an answer and makes a case for himself by telling Saul of previous acts of courage facing wild animals. The reasoning was simple – the same God who delivered David from a lion and bear would surely deliver him from the hands of the Philistines. Out of desperation, Saul agrees to let David fight Goliath.

Unfortunately, we tend to fight Goliath-size problems with a narrow human view, just as Saul did by dressing David in his own heavy armor. It wasn't long before David discarded the conventional approach and opted instead to rely solely on his faith in God for deliverance. David had complete trust in his God-given skills as he boldly approached Goliath with just five smooth stones and his sling. In short, David chose the armor of God over the armor of man, which is a lesson worth noting as we typically try to solve the problems we face with conventional methods instead of spiritual.

I find it interesting that David doesn't go to battle on just a "sling and a prayer." Instead, he first proclaims for all to hear that he comes to the fight in the name of the Lord Almighty who will hand Goliath over to him so the world will know there is a God in Israel. How fitting to make a public statement of faith before doing battle! While our settings will never be as dramatic as what is captured in I Samuel 17, we can be well served to proclaim our battles as those belonging to the Lord and not just our own. When we do, just as David did, we can take comfort knowing we are not alone, but instead are fighting along side God almighty, maker of Heaven and earth.

We know how the story ends, but I think it's important to point out that David didn't wait for Goliath to get within striking distance of his stones, but instead, verse 48 says David ran quickly toward the battle line to meet him. This description tells us David was approaching this fight with an expectant heart, fully trusting in God's victory. What would happen if we carried this same fearless mindset into our Goliath battles? I think it's worth a try because no battle is ever won by defending a position, but instead, by proactively advancing! If you are currently facing a Goliath in your life, it may be time to ask yourself what position you are taking, one of offense or defense.

When this day started for David, he had no idea that God would present before him a battle that would change his life forever. But it's fair to say that through David's faith and trust in his God and deliverer, he was ready to face Goliath with a fearless and expectant heart – a heart he would need when he became a king. While David didn't know God's plan for him on this given day, he knew to not be afraid and that the victory was his.

Through David's life-experiences, he captures the essence of living unafraid in Psalms 27 1-3:

The Lord is my light and my salvation – whom shall I fear?
The Lord is the stronghold of my life – of whom shall I be afraid?

When the wicked advance against me to devour me,
it is my enemies and my foes who will stumble and fall.

Though an army besiege me, my heart will not fear,
though war break out against me, even then I will be confident.

How confident are you of God's sovereign power? What victories await you when your heart is fearless and unafraid – victories that get you one step closer to fulfilling God's plan for your life?

Key Takeaways:

- God may place a Goliath in our lives when we least expect it, so we always need to be mindful and ready to respond with a fearless spirit.
- There will likely be detractors and naysayers when facing a Goliath and you will have to choose between listening to their critical voice or God's voice.
- We often forget to declare and turn over our battles to the Lord for Him to fight along side us.
- When facing a Goliath, we can either approach the problem passively with doubt or proactively with confidence.

Time of Reflection:

Is there a Goliath in your life that you are currently facing?

If there is, are you fighting this battle alone or with the Lord?

How would you describe the armor you have chosen to fight this problem?

Are you defending, hoping for the best outcome, or charging with a trusting heart?

Heavenly Father, I have no idea what today or tomorrow may bring, but I do know that whatever I face, I won't be alone. And, regardless of the size or nature of the problem, I am protected in Your armor and can face it with a fearless and expectant heart. Surround me, Lord, with the wisdom of Your word and the confidence of Your love.

10

TAKE COURAGE

Matthew 14:27 (Jesus to the Disciples)

*But Jesus immediately said to them: "Take courage! It is I. **Don't be afraid.**"*

Billy Graham once said, "courage is contagious." I wholeheartedly agree and believe this truth can have a profound impact on us all. It reminds me of one of my favorite movie scenes featuring Mel Gibson in *The Patriot*. Near the end of the film there is an epic battle of what would become the last stand between the colonial militia fighting for freedom and the well-trained and disciplined British army. During this climatic ending, when all hope seems lost, Mel Gibson's character courageously picks up the American flag that was abandoned during a full retreat and starts running back toward the enemy, giving the impression the momentum had swung over to the side of the over-matched militia. This act of courage contagiously inspires and renews the fighting spirit of his fellow soldiers and they ultimately overpower the British forces.

Since there are countless acts of courage happening every day, in every setting and walk of life, I thought a book on being unafraid should certainly address the topic of courage. Is being courageous the same as being fearless? If they are different, how so? For the most part, I believe there are many similarities between these character traits and they could be used interchangeably. However, I can also make the case that being fearless and unafraid, as addressed so far in this book, is more of a mindset or way of living. In comparison, courage could be viewed as an act of bravery or a rising up to a special calling or occasion. Several times, Jesus commanded his disciples to "take courage" or to take the action of being courageous.

I find acts of courage to be very inspiring, yet humbling because they bring to light the many times in my life when I've lacked courage when it was needed most. There are many high profile and low profile figures in the Bible who provide wonderful examples of courage and I would like to visit a couple of them.

The story of the baby Moses found floating in a basket down the Nile by Pharaoh's daughter is a children's classic that is often depicted in pictures and played out in church dramas. In this very familiar story, there is another character often overlooked for her act of courage. In Exodus 2, we read about the Levite woman who gave birth to a son, and when he was three months old, she put him in a basket among the reeds along the banks of the Nile. In verse 4, we learn that Miriam, the baby's older sister, not the mother, kept watch over the basket as it floated among the reeds. While we don't know how long Miriam stood watching to see what would happen, it's fair to assume she was alone and probably in unfamiliar territory.

As if being alone keeping watch over her baby brother wasn't courageous enough, Miriam was bold beyond her years when faced with what happened next. The Pharaoh's daughter discovers the basket, uncovers Moses and determines he is one of the Hebrew babies that her father ordered to be killed. When Miriam notices that the Pharaoh's daughter takes an interest in her baby brother, she courageously approached her with a brilliant idea. In verse 7, Miriam says, "Shall I go and call you a nurse from the Hebrew women to nurse the child for you?" So not only is Moses returned to his actual mother, but Pharaoh's daughter pays Miriam's mother to nurture her own son. Bold and brilliant!

When was the last time you had a courageous idea but didn't follow through because of fear that it would fail or you may be embarrassed? What if Miriam didn't have the courage to act on her quick thinking? I've heard the story of Moses in a basket so many times, but until recently, I've never really appreciated the courage of his sister. For those of you, like me, with a big sister who has faithfully watched over you, let her know how much she is appreciated!

You know someone is important when an entire book of the Bible is named after them -- Esther certainly deserves this high honor. In a quick summary, Esther was a beautiful Jewish queen of the Persian king, who courageously risked her life to save the Jewish nation from an evil plot by Haman, one of the King's top advisors. Esther did not take her courageous act lightly, and before intentionally breaking the King's law, she asked her cousin Mordecai to gather all the Jews in Susa to pray and fast for her for three days. Her act of courage was anything but spontaneous as she, along with her maids, also fasted for three days. Clearly, this remarkable woman believed in the power of going to God first with any major undertaking. Is that how you make key decisions or approach major events in your life? While I'm not advocating the practice of fasting for three days, when your life could be on the line, why not? Whatever you do, it's important to get your heart right with God, and to seek His will, not necessarily yours, before taking significant actions in your life.

Whether courage comes as a spontaneous act like that of Miriam, or a well-planned action bathed in prayer, like that of Esther, I believe acts of courage are game-changers that wait for their moment in the hearts of fearless and faithful people.

Key Takeaways:

- To "take courage" is making a conscious decision to rise up to the occasion at hand.
- Acts of courage are contagious when observed by others and can change the coarse of action.
- When undertaking a courageous act, bring it before the Lord and seek His will and blessing.

Time of Reflection:

When was the last time you witnessed a courageous act?

Did this action have any impact on others who observed it?

When was the last time you felt moved to act courageously, but chose not to, and why?

Heavenly Father, it's with a humble heart and weak spirit that I bow before You. My instinct is to run for shelter instead of stand for righteousness, yet my desire is to make a positive difference and to be a blessing to others. Give me the strength, Lord, to stand firm in my convictions and to take courage in my actions. May these acts of courage be a source of encouragement for others.

11

PAYING THE PRICE

Numbers 14:9 (Joshua to Israel)

*Only do not rebel against the Lord. And **do not be
afraid** of the people of the land, because we will
swallow them up. Their protection is gone, but the
Lord is with us. **Do not be afraid** of them.*

Fear and courage have always played a defining role in history,
and there are few times when this was more evident than when 12
leaders, one from each tribe of Israel, were sent out to explore the
promised land of Canaan. With this assignment, Moses gave them
specific instructions to see what the land and people were like. He
wanted to know about the soil, was it fertile or inadequate? Were
there trees and if so, what kind of fruit did they produce? How
about the people who lived there – were they strong or weak, few
or many, and were the towns open or fortified?

Just imagine all the questions the Israelites might have had about
this wondrous land that God had been promising them for so many
generations. After 40 days of following Moses' instruction, the
explorers returned and reported to the whole assembly. Just as God
had promised, they described the land as flowing with milk and
honey…which was the *good* news. The *bad* news was the land
was occupied by tribes who were powerful and lived in large,

fortified cities. This caused much fear and grumbling among the people.

Seeing this, Caleb, one of the 12, silenced the assembly in order to make his case for taking possession of this rich and bountiful, God-promised land. After all, that's the reason they were there at this place, at this time. However, most of the other explorers rejected Caleb's idea and had a much different opinion, saying, "Israel would surely be devoured by the much larger and stronger people." So, despite all the good reasons for entering this land, a land that God had clearly said was reserved for them, the people focused on all the talk about giants and fortified cities. Fear had its powerful grip once again.

The Israelites raised their voices, wept aloud and grumbled against Moses and Aaron. In turn, Caleb and Joshua were enraged and cried out to the entire assembly, "If the Lord is pleased with us, he will lead us into that land, a land flowing with milk and honey, and will give it to us. Only do not rebel against the Lord. And do not be afraid of the people of the land, because we will swallow them up. Their protection is gone, but the Lord is with us. Do not be afraid of them."

Unfortunately, their pep talk was unsuccessful and the people were about to stone them, when the glory of God appeared at the Tent of Meeting. I'm sure at that moment more than a few of the grumbling Israelites were second-guessing their response. And they should have been, as the Lord told Moses His plans to strike them down and destroy them all with a plague. Had Moses not interceded on Israel's behalf, begging for mercy, God was ready to start over making the family of Moses into a great nation, instead of using the descendents of Abraham.

The nation of Israel was spared, but there was a significant price to be paid for their disobedience. In particular, everyone who grumbled against the Lord, age 20 years or older, would never see the promised land, eventually perishing in the desert. The remaining Israelites would have to endure the desert wandering another 40 years before finally entering the promised land. By the way, the other 10 men who explored the land, but were afraid to join Joshua and Caleb, were struck down with a plague and died immediately before the Lord.

What a turning point! Instead of taking possession of a promised land flowing with milk and honey that had been Israel's entire objective since leaving Egypt, God's people lacked faith and became afraid. Their fear brought them to the brink of total destruction. Often, we do the same thing. We trust God to handle the smaller issues, but doubt his ability to take care of the big problems and frightening situations. When things get hairy, we can't stop trusting God just as we're about to reach our goals. We must remember all that God has done for us and let him complete His work in us.

Key Takeaways:

- Through fear, we tend to limit what is possible and quickly forget that if God is for us, no one can stand against us.

- Being afraid not only keeps us from experiencing all that God has planned for us, but it also reflects a disobedient heart that can lead to other sin in our lives.

- There are serious consequences to fearing man over God.

Time of Reflection:

Was there a time you were led by God to do something, but didn't because you were afraid?

As a result of your failure to act, did you lose out on an opportunity or were you penalized?

Is there something now in your life that you are being called to do, but you are afraid to act on it?

Heavenly Father, please forgive me for my lack of faith and lack of trust in the wonderful plan You have laid out before me. As I wander in the desert of my own desires, and focus on myself, give me courage to embrace the land You have promised me. Help me seize each day to bring glory to You and not myself.

THE GREAT COMMAND

12

FEARLESS IN FACING DEATH

Isaiah 44:2 (The Lord to Jacob)

This is what the Lord says, he who made you, who formed you in the womb, and who will help you: Do not be afraid, Jacob, my servant, whom I have chosen.

Why is it that people who have faced a near-death experience, or have overcome a life-threatening medical condition, like cancer, seem to live their days with such clarity and passion? There are countless stories of survivors who have turned their ordinary lives into extraordinary ones with meaning and purpose. I believe there are two common drivers behind this life-changing experience, that for many, become a blessing in disguise.

The first is a realization that nothing could be scarier than looking death in the eyes. Having stared down death, with death being the first to blink, a cancer survivor says, "Bring it on baby, you can't scare me!" After standing toe-to-toe with death, the uncertainties of life are simply not that big of a deal. Common things like proposing a new idea at work, confronting a family member about a sensitive topic, or even reaching out to a new neighbor all seem like slam dunk opportunities.

Fortunately, I have not had the experience of hearing my doctor use the "C" word, having my hair fall out in the shower, treating fragile areas of skin burned by radiation, examining a scar on a disfigured body part, or worse yet, looking into the hopeless eyes of my distraught family. But I can only imagine that everything else in life pales in comparison.

The second reality when facing death is the realization of just how precious and short our time is on earth. And when we see the sand quickly slipping through our own life's hourglass, the grains of sand suddenly change from an infinite number to something that's very measurable. At this point, a question arises that I believe everyone, who is given the opportunity, will ask at some point -- "Did I make the most of this very short life?"

The answer is most always "No!" So, a person who's given a second chance won't settle for idle time. Instead they're driven to make the most of the life that is represented by a mere dash mark on the tombstone that separates their date of birth from their date of death. How odd it seems that one's existence on earth, how ever long, is permanently etched in stone by a simple mark of such insignificance. Or is it?

If you were to die today, what story lies behind the dash on your tombstone? Will it simply be a mark that separates two dates, or will it represent a life of pursuit and purpose driven by a fearless attitude to seize each and every day God gives us?

One of the many things that I seem to tuck into the folds of my Bible is a simple inventory of things that I want to be, do, have, help and leave. Over the years, I've made some adjustments so it represents a current listing of my life's pursuits. Below is an example of some of the things on my list.

BEFORE I DIE, I WANT TO...

Be	Do	Have	Help	Leave
A grandfather who reads Bible stories to his grandchildren at bedtime	Dance with my daughter Libby on her wedding day	A small business with my wife Lori or a friend	Empower people to be: - Fearless - Themselves - A positive difference	A godly legacy and a good name for my children and their children
An author of a book that honors God and changes lives	A long weekend motorcycle trip with my sons Colby & Connor	A sporty convertible (*Yes, I lust over material things*)	My extended family and friends when they need me	My family financially secure

Today in the United States, the average life expectancy is approximately 74 years for a male and 80 years for a female. On a weekly basis, that means men live on average 3,848 weeks and women 4,160 weeks.

To provide a visual representation or reminder of my limited time on earth, Lori once gave me a unique gift for my new office – a large cookie jar made of clear glass, filled with colorful marbles. The marbles in the jar represented the approximate number of weeks remaining in my life. Because I was 46 at the time, there were only 1,456 precious marbles in the jar (74 – 46 = 28 years x 52 weeks).

While the marble jar made a striking decorative piece in my office, its purpose was much more significant. It was "interactive," because this gift came with instructions to remove one marble each Monday morning when I entered my office. By doing this, I was essentially removing one week of my life. This is pretty sobering when you think about it. But I found that two questions came to mind each week when a marble was removed. The first, "Did I make the most of the week I must now remove from the jar?" And the next obvious question was, "What will I do with the dwindling number of remaining weeks?"

Many times, as I held that little marble between my fingers and pondered the past week, I had difficulties with the truthful answers to these tough questions:

Did I make a positive difference in the lives of others?

Did I use my discretionary time wisely and with family?

Did I grow closer to the Lord or was my spiritual walk complacent?

Did I trust in God's plan and provision for my life?

Ultimately, the sobering answers were driven by whether I lived my life unafraid or afraid. Eventually, as one observes over time the dwindling number of marbles in the jar, questions like these bring greater consequences and clarity.

I think this is why, after walking through the fire of fighting for life, cancer survivors can't imagine living any other way but unafraid. They are forever reminded that facing death is a powerful experience for living life unafraid and focused. It's a reality check on how our time is so limited. The lesson to be learned is you don't have to fight for your life in order to approach it with a mindset of living unafraid over the "small stuff."

Key takeaways:

- It is a privilege to be living this day because it's a precious gift, and we should be mindful to live each day to the fullest, and by doing so make it holy.
- We don't need a terminal illness to transform ordinary living into a life with extraordinary benefits and blessings.
- Identify what is truly important to you. Then, be intentional about applying your time and energy towards these essential things.
- The fact of life is you are terminal, and it's time to start living like you were dying.

Time of Reflection:

When in your life have you most appreciated the gift of each day, and why?

Do you know anyone who has faced death and their perspective on life wasn't changed?

List the top three things that you want to do or accomplish in your lifetime, but haven't yet?

If you learned you had just 30 days to live, what would you do?

Heavenly Father, thank You for giving me another day and the wisdom to cherish it as the gift You intended it to be, and help me not be discouraged by disappointments along the way. Remove my petty worries, self-doubt and critical spirit. Lift the blinding fog of negativity so my eyes and heart can see opportunities to make a positive difference. Lord, keep me from sabotaging Your plan for me through debilitating fear and instead help me live like the next day will be my last.

13

FEARLESS OR FLAWLESS

Matthew 1:20 (Angel of the Lord to Joseph)

*But after he had considered this, an angel of the Lord appeared to him in a dream and said, "Joseph son of David, **do not be afraid** to take Mary home as your wife, because what is conceived in her is from the Holy Spirit."*

Following Christmas in 2008, our family went on a one-week vacation in Mexico. It was a wonderful time together that produced another collection of fond memories. One memory in particular captures the beauty of how uniquely different God made each of our children, and the self-imposed limits placed by people who are considered "perfectionists."

This was the setting – it was December 29, midway through our vacation and also the 20th birthday of Connor, our middle child. We were aboard a large ferry in the early evening headed back to the mainland after a fun-filled day on an off-shore island. Given the special occasion, I shared with the captain that he had a passenger on board who was celebrating a birthday. The captain was noticeably excited about this and was eager to accommodate his passenger's request to make a simple birthday wish over the boat's intercom.

Up to that point all was good, but unfortunately Connor noticed and overheard the tail end of my conversation with the captain when I looked his direction and said, "He's the one with the white sunglasses." Connor quickly connected the dots and gave me a look that screamed, "Dad, tell me you didn't really do that? Don't sell me out for the amusement of everybody else on this ferry!" Clearly, he wasn't going to play the role of a bashful birthday boy who didn't want a lot of attention – he was down-right mad and threatened to find the most remote corner of the ferry. Feeling somewhat guilty and second guessing my good intentions, I assured him that nothing would happen other than having his name announced over the intercom.

Have I mentioned that Connor is a perfectionist? While he is very accomplished and has experienced notable success and recognition at a young age, he is very uncomfortable in circumstances that are outside his control. He certainly doesn't like to fail. It's important to Connor to always put his best foot forward, which is another of his admirable traits, along with his ability to solve problems and think outside the box.

Just when I thought I'd calmed him down, Edgar, the captain of the ferry, came onto the intercom to cover some housekeeping notes to all passengers, after which he followed through with my request and announced it was Connor's birthday. What I didn't realize is Connor had given his white sunglasses to his older brother, Colby, who was sitting next to him. Immediately Connor started pointing to his good-natured sibling. And without hesitation, Colby bailed out his younger brother, like he had done numerous times before, raising his hand to acknowledge the crowd, and playing the role of birthday boy. However, much to Colby's surprise, that's not all the captain had in mind.

Captain Edgar thought it would only be appropriate to play the *Happy Birthday* song, encouraging the entire boatload of passengers to join in. Being the good sport that Colby is, he stood up to thank the large crowd on the upper deck, which also happened to be where the ferry had a makeshift dance floor. Feeling that the energy level of the passengers building, Edgar proceeded to play the ever-popular party dance tune, *Macarena*, and insisted (along with other passengers) the birthday boy go to the center platform, encircled by strangers sitting around the perimeter of the boat.

Needless to say, Colby was not expecting this! This was clearly not part of the plan when he agreed to take some of the heat off his younger brother. But, in response to the crowd's chanting encouragement and to their delight, Colby continued to play along and began dancing the *Macarena*, struggling to keep his balance aboard the tipsy ferry. The funny thing is, not too long after Colby made it clear he was having plenty of fun, others began to join him on the soon-to-be-filled dance floor. Complete strangers were having the time of their lives.

What's the message here? Because Colby "gets it," his fearlessness was contagious and inspired others to step out of their comfort zone to enjoy a part of the journey they had never anticipated. As I watched people that night, only a portion were willing to say, "I don't care what strangers think, I'm going to enjoy this opportunity to have fun."

While Connor found great enjoyment watching his brother's performance, there was no question in my mind which of the two enjoyed the moment more, and which brought more joy to those around them. The ferry ride would have ended as an uneventful trip, and nobody would have thought otherwise had Colby remained seated.

One of the ironies I later considered is Connor's ability to entertain and dance. He is actually very gifted in these areas, but simply feared the circumstances aboard the ferry. At dinner that night, when alone with Colby, I congratulated him on "getting it." He understood the meaning of living unafraid and received the joy and blessings that came with it. I then asked him what it was like. He summed it up in one word, "Awesome!" He went on to say it was some of the most fun he's ever had. It's worth noting this memorable experience came only as a result of Colby's spontaneous response to his brother's request. As a father, I was hoping this fearless example by the older brother was not lost on the younger brother, the perfectionist.

Key Takeaways:

- Being a perfectionist and not going outside our comfort zone can keep us from experiencing all that God has planned for us.
- Living unafraid can be contagious and inspiring to others. This is a wonderful gift to friends or family members, and even strangers that God puts in your path.
- Staying safe and precise can keep us from using the gifts and talents that God has given us.

Time of Reflection:

Do you feel like everything you do is a reflection of your value and worth?

The last time you did something below your expectations, how severe were the consequences?

What gift or talent would you like to exercise more, but haven't recently and why?

Heavenly Father, release me from my obsession with self and free me from the judgment of others. Lord, help me to live in the moment, to laugh at my mistakes and see myself as You see me. My worth is found only in You and not in what I do. My work and good fruit should be a testament to Your name and not mine.

14

LEAVING A LEGACY

Matthew 10:28 (Jesus to the Disciples)

Do not be afraid of those who kill the body but cannot kill the soul. Rather, be afraid of the One who can destroy both soul and body in hell.

It was a typical August morning in 1992 when I received an unexpected call from a family friend who began the conversation with, "Brad, I'm sorry, but I have some very bad news. Your dad passed away this morning." While I don't remember much else said after those few words, it was the start of a constant stream of memories, thoughts and emotions that I processed over the following weeks. Fortunately, I was blessed during this time with many prayers, words of condolences and notes of encouragement. However, there was one note in particular that caught my attention.

This short, hand-written note was from a friend who never met my father, but made the case for knowing him through me. This friend wrote about the value and importance of one's heritage and how our children are often our most visible and telling legacy. During this time of reflection about life, death and certainly my own mortality, I was forced to consider the fabric of my legacy. What will it look like? Will there be a defining accomplishment or will it be insignificant? There were a multitude of questions, but I kept coming back to what would be the legacy I'd be leaving my children?

For those of you who are parents and grandparents, I encourage you to address these questions with a sense of urgency, if you haven't yet. For some of you, the answer will be quite obvious. But for most of us it will require some intentional thinking. For those who may be tempted to arrive at a quick conclusion, you will be well served to give this careful consideration.

Our culture today, while with good intentions, gives far too much weight to the material things or the list of achievements we leave behind. For some, a lifetime is spent saving and hording money so an impressive estate can be left to their children, allowing them to live a life of comfort and luxury. Perhaps it's so their lives can be remembered for the hard work, frugal spending and commitment to children. While these are arguably admirable traits, money and material things will not equip our children or grandchildren for the challenges of life and the promises of eternity.

When I think about what legacy I want to leave my children, I certainly hope I'll be remembered as providing a good model and equipping them for life here on earth, but most importantly for eternal life in heaven. In reality, however, by pointing them to Jesus , I will have prepared them for both. It pains me to think of my children living a life shackled by fear, obsessed by what others think instead of what their Lord and Savior thinks. I don't want them to live a life of "what-ifs" knowing they passed up key relationships, new experiences and following God's will, all for the sake of playing it safe.

When I think of the legacy Jesus left for us, being fearful and playing it safe are not two descriptions that come to mind. Instead, I see a life lived through sacrificial and fearless love. It's never too late to influence the lasting legacy you want to leave. Do not be afraid to try, regardless of your past. If you are looking for a place to start building your legacy, I encourage you to start with sharing God's great command, "do not be afraid," with those you love. Share your knowledge that God gave this command more than any other in the Bible. Explain why He did this – so His children could experience a full and prosperous life, just like you want your children to live.

I believe if a national poll was taken to ask parents a question about their children's future, the vast majority would say, the choices and decisions to be made by their children will only be more challenging. I can't help but think in the global world we live in today, filled with unrest and hate, with unstable governments and fragile economies, the stakes will only keep rising. That's why, when I ponder my legacy, I want it to be one of teaching and modeling for my children the importance of living unafraid through my faith in Christ. I hope you'll consider the same!

Key Takeaways:

- Take inventory of what your legacy will be and start reshaping what needs attention.
- Our culture puts emphasis on what we leave, but it should be placed on "who" we leave.
- As the future becomes more uncertain, the importance of your legacy becomes more certain.

Time of Reflection:

If your funeral were tomorrow, what would your friends and family say about you?

Does your family know what is most important to you, and what you desire for them?

How can you help equip those you love, to be more fearless and live unafraid?

Heavenly Father, help me recognize how short my time on earth really is and where my priorities need to be. Forgive me when I get caught up in all the worldly trappings, when my greatest reward is the family You have entrusted to me. Lord, give me wisdom to be mindful of the legacy I leave and may it be honoring to You and my children.

15

OVERCOMING FEAR

Joshua 1:9 (God to Joshua before leading Israel into the promised land)

*Have I not commanded you? Be strong and courageous. **Do not be afraid,** do not be discouraged, for the Lord your God will be with you wherever you go.*

Fear can be a toxic emotion that creates a type of junkyard dog in our mind – a beast that viciously devours self-confidence, shreds our spirit, weakens our will and intimidates us from being our best, possibly even keeping us from trying at all. Unfortunately, the junk that fills our lives with busyness and the garbage that our culture defines as important, all contribute to feeding the bad dog of doubt and fear. It's impossible to totally kill the fear-filling animal within us, but we can certainly weaken it by simply feeding our faith and nourishing the Holy Spirit. In other words, it's logical to assume the one we feed most will increase its influence on our life.

So when someone asks me how to become unafraid, I break it down into a few simple pieces, that are geared towards one purpose: To starve fear and feed your faith. In order to starve your fear, you need to acknowledge its influence on your life and recognize when it's impacting even the simple decisions you are making. I hope the proceeding chapters have helped, however the question remains, "How do we starve the fear that dwells within us so we can feed our faith and become more fearless?"

Living unafraid is a continual process of feeding and exercising a fearless spirit through a faith in Jesus Christ as your savior. Just like our physical bodies are a reflection of what we eat and how we exercise, our mindset and approach to life is also directly impacted by what we feed our heart and how we exercise our faith.

#1: BEING KEENLY AWARE

While there are several key components to living unafraid, I believe it must begin with a keen awareness of how fear impacts our life every day. When we're not aware, it's so easy to slip into the same pattern of missed opportunities and blessings, allowing us to stumble and fall short of God's plan for our lives. Being aware doesn't have to be a difficult, complex thing – whenever we're faced with a choice, we just need to ask, "Why did I choose to act or not act and was this choice influenced by fear?" If fear was involved, ask yourself two simple questions. The first is, "What is the worst thing that could happen…is this outcome significantly greater than the potential benefit?" The second key question is, "Did I just pass up a blessing in disguise or a path that God put before me?"

It's so easy to slip into our daily routines. I encourage you to start each day with a challenge to live your life fearlessly instead of fearfully. This could either be said out loud, so you can hear yourself speak these words, or simply in prayer as you begin your day in communion with God. Challenge yourself to live the day like it was your last day, with no regret over missed opportunities.

I often lose track of God's command to not be afraid. When I first realized how fear limited the possibilities in my life, I would get frustrated with myself for falling into the same "comfort" trap. I knew the truth about how fear kept me from living a more fulfilling life, yet I continued to yield to my self-imposed insecurities. It was so disappointing! As I wrestled for answers and searched for some type of remedy, God placed on my heart to find a daily reminder of his command, "Do not be afraid." I needed something that kept this life-changing truth front and center in my life.

Little did I realize, the perfect solution I was seeking, would eventually be worn by many others. Here's the rest of the story. After weeks of considering how best to remind myself to live unafraid, I found the answer on a website. I could order 100 black rubber wristbands, stamped with "DO NOT BE AFRAID" in bold letters. (These wristbands are now available at the website **www.livingunafraid.com**.) Whether it's a simple rubber band around your wrist or a cross in your pocket, it's helpful to have a constant reminder of fear's impact on your life. It's the first, critical step to living unafraid.

#2: Feeding Your Faith

As discussed earlier, there is a constant warfare between one's faith and fear. When one is strong, the other is weak...very simple, but very true. And because fear is always present and a part of how we're wired, it requires an intentional effort for each of us to exercise and strengthen our faith. By doing so and by feeding our faith, we are starving and weakening fear's grip on us.

How does a person feed their faith? It's a short, straightforward question, but the answer can be a bit more complicated because it's very personal for each of us. However, I would suggest there are some universal methods.

Get to know God personally by spending regular time reading and understanding scripture, remembering this is His love letter to you. How many love letters have you received, but never read? For most of us, a love letter is poured over from beginning to end multiple times as we hang on the meaning of each word. Our heavenly father desires the same thing of his earthly children. Through scripture, we learn who God is, how He wants us to live, and His plan for us to spend eternity with Him.

In addition to frequently being in the word of God, we need to be in the company of God. We need to seek His face and voice through an undivided time of prayer. God created us for fellowship and worship with Him and both are achieved through prayer. It's a time of sharing your heart, seeking His wisdom and listening for His voice and direction. Without this time with God, it is impossible to understand His will and purpose for your life.

Because we are often surrounded by conflicting and negative influences on our lives, it is also important to surround ourselves in positive fellowship with others. Beyond just going to church and spending an hour with other "church goers," we need extended fellowship with fellow believers. Do you have a circle of people who exhibit Christ's love and speak truth? Do you interact with others who share an eternal perspective and remind you of what is truly important? Or are those around you focused more on how they look, their social status or the material things that bring them temporary happiness?

As a parent, I was always very aware of and interested in the friendships of my three children. The reason is simple – the people around us significantly shape who we are and will be. While this truth especially applies to young people, it still holds true for people of all ages – it certainly applies to influencers of our faith.

#3: Keeping an Eternal Perspective

If you have ever played sports, you are very familiar with the importance of focus and concentration. As a kid growing up playing baseball, I remember my father coaching me with the words, "Keep your eye on the ball." When playing basketball, it was, "Keep your eye on the front of the rim." Success in either sport required focusing on the ball or the rim. The same is true with the way we live our lives. In order to live with focus and purpose, we need to identify what is truly most important to us. While many people spend a lifetime trying to figure this out chasing possessions, popularity or power, Christians believe eternity is what matters most.

Why is eternity the single most important thing to Christians? In addition to being the cornerstone of the Christian faith, the answer to this question centers on being reunited with God, family and friends in an unimaginably beautiful place called heaven. This sounds great, but I left out one key word – forever. It's difficult for humans to comprehend what forever really means, but maybe an illustration will help. Regardless of how long someone lives, whether it's 18 or 88 years, life on earth is just one dot compared to an eternal line that never ends.

So what does it mean to keep an eternal perspective? Think about this. If our entire life is but a dot compared to an eternal line that never ends, why do we become fearful and get caught up in moments of worrying about how we look, or what we say? Why do we fear rejection and failure when we know God has a plan for us? And we know from scripture that no person or endeavor will keep us from eternity in heaven. If we stayed focused on the fact that eternity is all that really matters and nothing else is more important, we don't need to sweat the small stuff of life that our culture says is important. Whether it's a big promotion you didn't get, not being included with friends or not making a school team – none of these things "within the dot" can keep you from heaven.

#4: Perfect Love

1 John 4:18 states it best, "There is no fear in love, and perfect love drives out fear." While clearly stated, you may wonder what is perfect love? To give you a hint, much of 1 John speaks of who Jesus is as our savior. When John defines Jesus, he speaks of Him in terms of sacrificial and selfless love. So perfect love is an outward love with a focus on others and not on self, which makes it completely selfless and sacrificial. While Christ is our model of selfless and sacrificial love, this type of perfect love is demonstrated countless times every day. The most identifiable example is a mother's love. A love that is so outwardly focused on the care of her children, there is little regard for her own wellbeing, even to the point of putting herself at risk with no hesitation or fear. How many stories have you heard about a mother instinctively putting herself, sacrificially, in harm's way to protect her child? In each situation, there is a common theme or action as a result of a mother's perfect and selfless love – and fear is not present.

My point is this. It is impossible to be fearless when we are focused on ourselves and our love is focused solely inward. We're absorbed in how we look, sound and feel and we fear everything that could tarnish or hinder any of our self-centered emotions. If you find yourself feeling fearful, stop and examine where your love and attention is directed. It may be more inward than you realize. Believe me, I say this from first-hand experience.

Like any endeavor or goal that is worthwhile, living unafraid will not happen overnight. It's a life-changing pursuit. It's a journey and you cannot let yourself be discouraged by periods when you'll have to battle a fearful spirit.

Please take heart, persevere and stay focused on:

- Fear's influence on your life
- Feeding your faith in Christ
- Keeping an eternal perspective
- Loving outwardly and sacrificially

Rest assured, you'll struggle with some of these goals more than others, and you may falter at times in one or two areas. There's no doubt, you will be challenged along your journey. Just remember, they are collectively the foundation to living unafraid. Should you find yourself struggling with a fearful spirit, do not be discouraged as we are reminded in Joshua 1:9 of His command and promise:

> *Have I not commanded you? Be strong and courageous. Do not be discouraged and do not be afraid, for the Lord your God will be with you wherever you go.*

When you find yourself standing on the edge of the pool and the deep water of life seems scary and uncertain, take heart. Your heavenly father has His arms stretched toward you and calls your name, saying "Look at me and keep your eyes on me. Trust me and do not be afraid. I will not let anything happen to you and I have a plan for you. I will never leave you or forsake you."

WWW.LIVINGUNAFRAID.COM

10 Truths of Living Unafraid

We've covered a lot of ground on the topic of living unafraid, and I trust a few personal and biblical stories sprinkled with scripture have provided some thought-provoking reading. There are 10 truths that I want to close with before you put this book down, or share it with someone you care about. My hope is you never lose sight of these truths in your life-changing pursuit to live unafraid through your faith in Jesus, our Lord and Savior.

1. God commands his children more than any other in the Bible to "Do not be afraid."

2. Living unafraid is not an overnight change, but a lifelong journey requiring continuous awareness and courage.

3. Fear and faith are two driving forces within each person that are constantly at odds vying for control. When we feed one, the other starves.

4. Peter was fearless as he stepped out of the boat and walked on the water, but when he took his eyes off Jesus and saw the wind, he became afraid.

5. The one thing we should fear most, is fearing the judgment of man over the judgment of God.

6. No battle is won by being defensive. When facing a Goliath, we can either approach the problem passively wearing the armor of man, or proactively wearing the armor of God.

7. If we desire to be obedient and do the right things, it starts with obedience to the Holy Spirit.

8. Being afraid not only keeps us from experiencing all that God has planned for us, but also reflects a disobedient heart that can lead to serious consequences.

9. Perfect love drives out fear and a selfless love that is sacrificial makes you unafraid.

10. Keep an eternal perspective and don't sweat the "life stuff." There is no awkward moment, no personal setback and certainly no other person's opinion that can keep you from what matters most, which is eternity with your heavenly father and family.

THE GREAT COMMAND
"DO NOT BE AFRAID"

VERSE	FROM	TO	SCRIPTURE
Genesis 15:1	The Lord	Abram	After this, the word of the Lord came to Abram in a vision: "Do not be afraid, Abram. I am your shield, your very great reward."
Genesis 21:17	Angel of God	Hagar	God heard the boy crying, and the angel of God called to Hagar from heaven and said to her, "What is the matter, Hagar? Do not be afraid; God has heard the boy crying as he lies there."
Genesis 26:24	The Lord	Isaac	That night the Lord appeared to him and said, "I am the God of your father Abraham. Do not be afraid, for I am with you; I will bless you and will increase the number of your descendants for the sake of my servant Abraham."
Genesis 46:3	God	Jacob	"I am God, the God of your father," he said. "Do not be afraid to go down to Egypt, for I will make you into a great nation there."
Numbers 21:34	The Lord	Moses	The Lord said to Moses, "Do not be afraid of him, for I have delivered him into your hands, along with his whole army and his land. Do to him what you did to Sihon king of the Amorites, who reigned in Heshbon."
Deuteronomy 1:21	The Lord	Israel	"See, the Lord your God has given you the land. Go up and take possession of it as the Lord, the God of your ancestors, told you. Do not be afraid; do not be discouraged."

VERSE	FROM	TO	SCRIPTURE
Deuteronomy 3:2	The Lord	Moses	The Lord said to me, "Do not be afraid of him, for I have delivered him into your hands, along with his whole army and his land. Do to him what you did to Sihon king of the Amorites, who reigned in Heshbon."
Joshua 1:9	The Lord	Joshua	"Have I not commanded you? Be strong and courageous. Do not be afraid; do not be discouraged, for the Lord your God will be with you wherever you go."
Joshua 8:1	The Lord	Joshua	Then the Lord said to Joshua, "Do not be afraid; do not be discouraged. Take the whole army with you, and go up and attack Ai. For I have delivered into your hands the king of Ai, his people, his city and his land."
Joshua 10:8	The Lord	Joshua	The Lord said to Joshua, "Do not be afraid of them; I have given them into your hand. Not one of them will be able to withstand you."
Joshua 11:6	The Lord	Joshua	The Lord said to Joshua, "Do not be afraid of them, because by this time tomorrow I will hand all of them, slain, over to Israel. You are to hamstring their horses and burn their chariots."
Judges 6:23	The Lord	Gideon	But the Lord said to him, "Peace! Do not be afraid. You are not going to die."
2 Kings 1:15	Angel of the Lord	Elijah	The angel of the Lord said to Elijah, "Go down with him; do not be afraid of him." So Elijah got up and went down with him to the king.
2 Kings 19:6	The Lord	King's Officials	Isaiah said to them, "Tell your master, 'This is what the Lord says: Do not be afraid of what you have heard—those words with which the underlings of the king of Assyria have blasphemed me.'"

VERSE	FROM	TO	SCRIPTURE
2 Chronicles 20:15	The Lord	Judah and Jerusalem	He said: "Listen, King Jehoshaphat and all who live in Judah and Jerusalem! This is what the Lord says to you: 'Do not be afraid or discouraged because of this vast army. For the battle is not yours, but God's.'"
2 Chronicles 20:17	The Lord	Judah and Jerusalem	"'You will not have to fight this battle. Take up your positions; stand firm and see the deliverance the Lord will give you, Judah and Jerusalem. Do not be afraid; do not be discouraged. Go out to face them tomorrow, and the Lord will be with you.'"
Isaiah 7:4	The Lord	Isaiah	"Say to him, 'Be careful, keep calm and don't be afraid. Do not lose heart because of these two smoldering stubs of firewood— because of the fierce anger of Rezin and Aram and of the son of Remaliah.'"
Isaiah 8:12,13	The Lord	Isaiah	"Do not call conspiracy everything this people calls a conspiracy; do not fear what they fear, and do not dread it. The Lord Almighty is the one you are to regard as holy, he is the one you are to fear, he is the one you are to dread."
Isaiah 41:10	God	Israel	"So do not fear, for I am with you; do not be dismayed, for I am your God. I will strengthen you and help you; I will uphold you with my righteous right hand."
Isaiah 41:13	The Lord	Israel	"For I am the Lord your God who takes hold of your right hand and says to you, Do not fear; I will help you."
Isaiah 41:14	The Lord	Israel	"Do not be afraid, you worm Jacob, little Israel, do not fear, for I myself will help you," declares the Lord, your Redeemer, the Holy One of Israel.

VERSE	FROM	TO	SCRIPTURE
Isaiah 43:5	The Lord	Israel	"Do not be afraid, for I am with you; I will bring your children from the east and gather you from the west."
Isaiah 44:2	The Lord	Jacob	"This is what the Lord says— he who made you, who formed you in the womb, and who will help you: Do not be afraid, Jacob, my servant, Jeshurun, whom I have chosen."
Isaiah 44:8	The Lord	Israel	"Do not tremble, do not be afraid. Did I not proclaim this and foretell it long ago? You are my witnesses. Is there any God besides me? No, there is no other Rock; I know not one."
Isaiah 54:4a	The Lord	Israel	"Do not be afraid; you will not be put to shame. Do not fear disgrace; you will not be humiliated."
Isaiah 57:11	God	Israel	"Whom have you so dreaded and feared that you have not been true to me, and have neither remembered me nor taken this to heart? Is it not because I have long been silent that you do not fear me?"
Jeremiah 1:8	The Lord	Judah	"Do not be afraid of them, for I am with you and will rescue you," declares the Lord.
Jeremiah 10:5	The Lord	House of Israel	"Like a scarecrow in a cucumber field, their idols cannot speak; they must be carried because they cannot walk. Do not fear them; they can do no harm nor can they do any good."
Jeremiah 30:10	The Lord	Israel	"'So do not be afraid, Jacob my servant; do not be dismayed, Israel,' declares the Lord. 'I will surely save you out of a distant place, your descendants from the land of their exile. Jacob will again have peace and security, and no one will make him afraid.'"

VERSE	FROM	TO	SCRIPTURE
Jeremiah 42:11	The Lord	Army Officers	"Do not be afraid of the king of Babylon, whom you now fear. Do not be afraid of him, declares the Lord, for I am with you and will save you and deliver you from his hands."
Jeremiah 46:27	The Lord	Israel	"Do not be afraid, Jacob my servant; do not be dismayed, Israel. I will surely save you out of a distant place, your descendants from the land of their exile. Jacob will again have peace and security, and no one will make him afraid."
Jeremiah 46:28a	The Lord	Israel	"Do not be afraid, Jacob my servant, for I am with you," declares the Lord. "Though I completely destroy all the nations among which I scatter you, I will not completely destroy you."
Jeremiah 51:46	The Lord	Israel	"Do not lose heart or be afraid when rumors are heard in the land; one rumor comes this year, another the next, rumors of violence in the land and of ruler against ruler."
Ezekiel 2:6	The Sovereign Lord	Ezekiel	"And you, son of man, do not be afraid of them or their words. Do not be afraid, though briers and thorns are all around you and you live among scorpions. Do not be afraid of what they say or be terrified by them, though they are a rebellious people."
Ezekiel 3:9	The Sovereign Lord	Ezekiel	"I will make your forehead like the hardest stone, harder than flint. Do not be afraid of them or terrified by them, though they are a rebellious people."
Daniel 10:12	The Lord	Daniel	Then he continued, "Do not be afraid, Daniel. Since the first day that you set your mind to gain understanding and to humble yourself before your God, your words were heard, and I have come in response to them."

Verse	From	To	Scripture
Daniel 10:19	The Lord	Daniel	"Do not be afraid, you who are highly esteemed," he said. "Peace! Be strong now; be strong." When he spoke to me, I was strengthened and said, "Speak, my lord, since you have given me strength."
Haggai 2:5	The Lord	Israel	"This is what I covenanted with you when you came out of Egypt. And my Spirit remains among you. Do not fear."
Zechariah 8:13	The Lord	Jerusalem	"Just as you, Judah and Israel, have been a curse among the nations, so I will save you, and you will be a blessing. Do not be afraid, but let your hands be strong."
Zechariah 8:15	The Lord	Jerusalem	"So now I have determined to do good again to Jerusalem and Judah. Do not be afraid."
Matthew 1:20	Angel of the Lord	Joseph	But after he had considered this, an angel of the Lord appeared to him in a dream and said, "Joseph son of David, do not be afraid to take Mary home as your wife, because what is conceived in her is from the Holy Spirit."
Matthew 10:26	Jesus	Disciples	"So do not be afraid of them, for there is nothing concealed that will not be disclosed, or hidden that will not be made known."
Matthew 10:28	Jesus	Disciples	"Do not be afraid of those who kill the body but cannot kill the soul. Rather, be afraid of the One who can destroy both soul and body in hell."
Matthew 28:5	Angel of the Lord	Mary Magdalen	The angel said to the women, "Do not be afraid, for I know that you are looking for Jesus, who was crucified."
Matthew 28:10	Jesus	Mary and Mary at the Tomb	Then Jesus said to them, "Do not be afraid. Go and tell my brothers to go to Galilee; there they will see me."

VERSE	FROM	TO	SCRIPTURE
Luke 1:13	Angel of the Lord	Zechariah	But the angel said to him: "Do not be afraid, Zechariah; your prayer has been heard. Your wife Elizabeth will bear you a son, and you are to call him John."
Luke 1:30	Angel of the Lord	Virgin Mary	But the angel said to her, "Do not be afraid, Mary; you have found favor with God."
Luke 2:10	Angel of the Lord	Shepherds	But the angel said to them, "Do not be afraid. I bring you good news that will cause great joy for all the people."
Luke 12:4	Jesus	Disciples	"I tell you, my friends, do not be afraid of those who kill the body and after that can do no more."
Luke 12:32	Jesus	Disciples	"Do not be afraid, for your Father has been pleased to give you the kingdom."
John 14:27	Jesus	Disciples	"Peace I leave with you; my peace I give you. I do not give to you as the world gives. Do not let your hearts be troubled and do not be afraid."
Acts 18:9	The Lord	Paul	One night the Lord spoke to Paul in a vision: "Do not be afraid; keep on speaking, do not be silent."
Acts 27:24	Angel of God	Paul	Do not be afraid, Paul. You must stand trial before Caesar; and God has graciously given you the lives of all who sail with you.
Revelations 1:17	Lord God	John	When I saw him, I fell at his feet as though dead. Then he placed his right hand on me and said: "Do not be afraid. I am the First and the Last."
Revelations 2:10	Lord God	Church of Smyrna	"Do not be afraid of what you are about to suffer. I tell you, the devil will put some of you in prison to test you, and you will suffer persecution for ten days. Be faithful, even to the point of death, and I will give you life as your victor's crown."

ABOUT THE AUTHOR

Brad Elmitt was born and raised in Des Moines, Iowa. He is the son of Bob and Alyce Elmitt, and is married to his best friend and lifelong love Lori (Colby) Elmitt. Brad is also the father of Colby, Connor and Libby who motivate him daily to be all that God called him to be. It is this calling that has inspired Brad to encourage others with God's great command, "Do not be afraid." In addition to writing this book, Brad has had the privilege of speaking to various groups of both adults and youth about what it means to honor God, seize each day and bless others by **living unafraid!**

Made in the USA
Charleston, SC
17 November 2015